PARALLEL LIVES

ACKNOWLEDGMENTS

The following poems previously have been published:
Parnassus: "Maragheh and Alamut"; *Poetry*: "When You Are Someone Else," "Certain Dark" and "They"; *The Hudson Review*: "Messengers" and "Silences"; *Partisan Review*: "On the Cherwell"; *Cimarron Review*: "Oak Wilt" and "Industrial Landscape"; *Nebraska Review*: "Jamaica," "Midnight to Noon," "The Land of Nod," "The Minor Prophets," and "The Photographer's Model"; *Sparrow*: "The World Outside"; *The Formalist*: "The Ballad of Woodrow Wilson" and "The Death of Seneca"; *Southern Humanities Review*: "Airport Prayer"; *Pivot*: "In the Confucian Temple in Hanoi," "Genesis," "Gliese 876," "The Day Is At An End," "Land of the Eastering Rivers," "For the Cold War Dead," "Cibola," "Maximilian's Eye" and "The Shooting at the Zoo"; *Hellas*: "Prothalamion: Tableau Vivant," *Edge City Review*: "American Athena"; *Neovictorian/Cochlea*: "Mount Wilson Observatory"; *Gadfly*: "The Siege of Dubrovnik, 1992."

"When You Are Someone Else," "Messengers," "Certain Dark" and "They" have also been collected in a chapbook, *When You Are Someone Else* (Aralia Press, 2002).

Etruscan Press
Wilkes University
84 West South Street
Wilkes-Barre, PA 18766
www.etruscanpress.org

Publisher's Cataloging-in-Publication

    Lind, Michael, 1962-
        Parallel lives / Michael Lind.
        p. cm.
        Poems.
        ISBN-13: 978-09745995-8-8
        ISBN-10: 0-9745995-8-1
        I. Title.
        PS3562.I482P37 2007   811'.54

Designed by Dinah Fried

The publication of Parallel Lives *has been made possible by a grant from the National Endowment for the Arts.*

NATIONAL
ENDOWMENT
FOR THE ARTS
A great nation
deserves great art.

PARALLEL LIVES
MICHAEL LIND

www.etruscanpress.org

CONTENTS

I

Maragheh and Alamut   9

II

When You Are Someone Else   17
On the Cherwell   18
The Hour   20
Messengers   21
Prothalamion: Tableau Vivant   23
Oak Wilt   25
Mount Wilson Observatory   27
The Minor Prophets   29
Airport Prayer   30
Industrial Landscape   31
Morning in Texas   32
Silences   33
The World Outside   34
Certain Dark   35

III

Parallel Lives   41

IV

For the Cold War Dead   53
Jamaica   56
Gliese 876   57
The Photographer's Model   58

Maximilian's Eye   59

The Glass Blower   60

Seventeen Year Cicada   61

This After   63

The Death of Pindar   64

The Land of Nod   65

They   67

V

The Judge   71

VI

American Athena   79

In the Confucian Temple in Hanoi   80

Cardinal Bembo's Epitaph for Raphael   81

Genesis   82

The Siege of Dubrovnik, 1992   84

The Shooting At the Zoo   85

Cibola   88

The Ballad of Woodrow Wilson   89

The Death of Seneca   91

Midnight to Noon   92

The Day is at an End   93

Land of the Eastering Rivers   94

Retrospective   95

I

MARAGHEH AND ALAMUT

I love a forest gap that a hike's disclosed
within an Appalachian maze of pine:
        a fractured column shines inside the
                chasm of daylight its fall created,

a cylinder of moss in an aureole
of ferns, lethargic flames. To the piney woods
        this weekend, to your mountain cabin,
                we will ascend from the sentried forum;

your invitation, Steve, is accepted. Let
reporters garble names on projected maps,
        while soldiers trap our enemies in
                caverns and canyons. In plusher mountains,

the talk will be of friends and relationships
and minor feuds and Washington real estate;
        and when the stripes of sky have darkened
                we will recline as the constellations

condense like drops that shingle an amber glass.
The earthly paradise is an odd, remote,
      extravagant observatory:
            Palomar's egg in its nest of needles,

or Tycho Brahe's island, Uraniborg,
or maybe Jaipur, sundial of the gods,
      where steps go slanting up a style that
            sunders an arch with its flooding shadow.

Or Maragheh. In what is today Iran,
atop a hill, the Persian astronomer
      al-Tusi, midway through the thirteenth
            century, built an observatory

with monstrous copper quadrants and astrolabes
and orreries depicting a universe
      where earth had rinds of sky. An adjunct
            library coffered Hellenic classics

of physics, math and medicine: Hypsicles
and Euclid, Archimedes and Ptolemy,
      whose Almagest acquired al-Tusi's
            trigonometric illuminations.

Al-Tusi, if the lore is to be believed,
had been a hostage once in the mountain fort
      of Alamut. The first Assassins
            there had a school for frontierless murder.

The captive might have witnessed how solemn boys
atop the Rock, when beckoned to by their lord,
      would glide across the sky, like divers
            arcing from clifftops in Acapulco.

From Alamut—like Maragheh, in Iran—
apostles of the holy fraternity
      diffused. Artistic daggers tinted
            halls in Damascus and squares in Baghdad.

Abbasid kings and Frankish crusaders broke.
At last Hulagu, grandson of Genghis Khan,
    with engineers from China joined by
        troops from Armenia, chose to martyr

the saints of Alamut. The subduers had
to torch the timber roofs of the catacombs.
    I've known that odor since November's
        visit to smoldering south Manhattan.

A legend says al-Tusi betrayed the fort.
In later years the Mongol, we know, would be
    attentive when the Persian showed him
        planets that flicker above your cabin.

Up there we'll scan for meteors, not for planes.
Each time I take Connecticut Avenue
    across the bridge, I'm trapped again with
        hundreds around me, evacuated

beneath the lamp-post eagles and powerless,
eroded lions, empire's regalia;
  we stride in silence, glancing upward
    briefly, compulsively. From our office

you could have seen the smoke from the Pentagon,
but you were at the Capitol, in a mob
  of Senators and staffers jumbled
    onto the steps by police. Above you

that morning in September a summit rose,
a hilltop dome which, but for a crater dug
  in Pennsylvania, might have crumpled,
    burying you in the burning columns.

The woods, this weekend, then. Let December end
with us upon your deck when the stars fill in
  the slots between the trees. And let us
    drink to al-Tusi and toast Hulagu.

.

      —Washington, D.C. December 2001

II

WHEN YOU ARE SOMEONE ELSE

When you are someone else perhaps we'll meet.
Some years from now, somebody with a face
like yours, but older, in some public place,
an airport maybe, or a city street,
will see someone resembling me. They'll greet
each other, knowing long ago, somewhere,
in other bodies, they had chanced to share
a momentary glow, a mortal heat.

I do not want to spend my lives with you,
nor can you speak for those whom you'll become.
The people who succeed us must be free
to choose the ones they love, the way that we
for now have chosen one another. Come,
before tomorrow makes me someone new.

ON THE CHERWELL

Old cultures, like old couples, learn
abbreviation, letting gesture serve
    in place of speech,
until the telling word may seem
itself a clot in silence, as a clean
    scrimshaw may leach

its lightness from the buoyant void.
Consider how a paper fan destroys
    the hero of
a Chinese opera, or think of with
what nuances of shrug this punter hints
    to friend, to love,

to us and other diners by
the bank tonight of sentiments too fine
    for tongue to mold,
communicated by his lift
and stance instead. The boat begins to pitch
    because he poled

flamboyantly; his passengers
rebuke him by inclining in the stern,
      straw brims the weights
adjusted on an orrery
that balances and reconciles these three
      old worlds. None prates,

none analyzes, all is shift
and countershift between the trees, black wicks,
      and waxen gold,
as gravities align around
the axis of this latest staff to plough
      the sifted mold.

THE HOUR

Maybe the moment recurs daily at six, when commuters,
        freed from the staring computers,
elbow and bump in unsought intimacy on a station
        platform with you, and frustration
rots what is left of your strength. Maybe the hour comes after
        dinner, when televised laughter
seeps from a neighboring room; maybe the time is the dead of
        night, when you ponder, instead of
dreaming. Whatever the time, you will escape it—by sinking
        down with a book, or by drinking
secretly out in the dark studio, or by unbuckling
        pants on a stranger, or chuckling,
one with a mob, in a deep theater. Soon, though, the hour
        comes to corrode all your power,
pleasure and faith with the damp dread that it daily assigns you.
        How you evade it defines you.

MESSENGERS

Abruptly, it will be
athwart the cornice, blinking
into my office—a sea gull,
a blowzy, prinking
apparition, like the skull
in Arcady, diverting reverie
to otherness—in this case, to marine
translucencies far from the fax machine.

Just so, the messengers
confound us in our practiced
routine, spooky as upstart flowers
in chalky, cactused
gullies. Oracle of powers,
a walkie-talkie simmers, crackles, purrs
direction to this haughty boy, whose smirk
might find its type in Botticelli's work;

a ripple follows him, through rows
of desks, as flexing muscles wrapped
in black-and-purple tights divert
the women and some men. He knows,
he must, that he is peeled by rapt
receptionists who seem so curt.

Conceited couriers!
—each advertised as peerless,
unique, by his heraldic garb;
this guy's a cheerless
Zulu ninja, dressed to perturb
in mask-like goggles; key-chains echo spurs
accompanying the swagger of that pard
whose look is Stetson, jersey, leotard.

Their uniforms mock ours,
our rep ties and our jackets
or overalls. They flaunt their grace,
these knights of packets
who bear down on us mid-race
outside on sidewalks at lunch hours,
a whoosh the only warning, not a bell,
and then we're nearly clipped. They spool, pell-mell,

through car-stampedes, they flag and tease
the snorting trucks, and pedal on
with order, deposition, plan,
kid brothers of Pheidippides,
the messenger of Marathon.
His heart stumbled, yet still he ran.

PROTHALAMION: TABLEAU VIVANT

For Kevin and Dana

The vaudeville curtain peels back from a frieze;
the footlights glaze a powdered Wedgewood thigh,
educing from the small-town crowd a sigh
that mingles awe and lust. The trembling knees
betray a less than classic strength and ease.

That was the fad, a century ago,
when actors would bring brushed or chiselled form
to languid life: a Grecian nymph, as warm
as blushing Galatea, troops who row
an emblematic Washington through snow.

To array ourselves in just such a tableau
we have convened. Here, mutability
will incarnate the types of harmony
and frame a passing fixity in flow.
This is a moment when, as in a Noh

performance, movement suddenly must slow,
arresting our attention, freeing us,
if only for an instant, from the press
of personality. Not what can grow,
but what has crystallized will be on show.

The ensemble's members, one by one, will drift
from their positions, marble eyes will blink,
the curtain drop, the statue reach for drink;
for now, a small forever, though, the gift
of ceremony has reduced the rift;

for now, the players gazing on a gold
fake apple are Minerva, Juno, fair
Queen Venus; now the smile-exchanging pair
preside at heaven's banquet. While we hold
this pose, the two are perfect, classic, cold.

OAK WILT

To be among the others, yet apart,
to be an element and still a whole,
to synchronize with other hearts a heart
pulsing for one alone—this is the goal

of animals like us. Our common life
is made from unities that link like chain
or like the live-oaks, knotted in slow strife,
that blackly web a yellow Texan plain.

Rising from roots that blend, a live-oak motte
is both a forest and a single tree.
Its wonders are the kind that can be wrought
only by an entire community:

cathedral panes of green, framed by the boughs
that buttress vaults where birds and squirrels nest,
the wicker-work arcades where deer can browse
in safety and where butterflies can rest.

Contagion kills commingled oaks at once.
From root to threaded root the wilt is spread
like public myth or tribal arrogance
until the dead prop up the standing dead.

Better to tempt the lightning in a field,
better to take a chance of being blown
to splinters without neighbors as a shield.
Though branches meet, let roots remain alone.

MOUNT WILSON OBSERVATORY

In France, the mirror's glass was poured
by bottle-makers. While the lens
in California would record
primeval glitter, Flemish fens
would crunch with glass when nations warred.

The titan looming once at Rhodes
was cast from siegers' melted arms;
just so, a shattered era's modes
are here remembered in the forms
of this colossus. See, the nodes

that stud the column's massive yoke
are rivets from a Yankee yard
that blended sweat and ore and coke
in battleships. The very art
that turned this instrument bespoke

the skill of those who sought to aim
a kindred barrel at a foe
horizons hid. Deep in the game,
a general smoked. A pipe would glow
beneath the dark reflector's frame.

Its armor parted, like a gun
the hundred-inch would whir to find
its targets. News that ours is one
of countless clusters undermined
our confidence more than Verdun.

THE MINOR PROPHETS

None of the minor prophets
knew that he was minor, of course. Habakkuk, I imagine,
    thought that his visions earned him
standing as Ezekiel's peer, if not indeed Elijah's.
    Then there was Obadiah,
who could be forgiven if he thought he might be a Moses.
    How they would be remembered
Providence concealed from them all, though they could see the future.

    Maybe it doesn't matter.
If you're on a mission from God, sent to rebuke a city
    or to redeem a nation,
where by canon-makers you're ranked may be inconsequential.
    Nor is the voice within you
any less authentic for not having a distant echo.
    Seers of the world, be heartened.
Even minor prophets can have genuine revelations.

AIRPORT PRAYER

May a current of shining air
rinse the eddies of dark smoke from transparency,
    lover, as you return. May winds
burst, as weak as champagne bubbles, against the sleek
    prow dividing the atmosphere.
Near the treetops, may clear breezes collect and may
    they, as porpoises in a school
nudge a swimmer to shore, shoulder you down once more.

INDUSTRIAL LANDSCAPE

Along the power line,
December trees define
    a grid
that green once hid;

the twigs, like wires on poles,
connect the naked boles.
    A thin
enamel skin

of recent snow's concealed
the grasses of the field
    near tubes
and concrete cubes.

The chimney-stacks emit
great cones of steam, which, it
    appears,
create the tiers

of cloud. The worlds of soil
and steel are one, of oil
    and trees
and factories.

MORNING IN TEXAS

Pasted on an eddy, the buzzards glisten
blackly, drifting over the cedar. This is
when you hear the rustle, and—if you listen
carefully—hisses.

SILENCES

The quiet that expands, like the mist that glides
from valleys up the forested mountainsides
      until each summit of a highland
            range is a separate silver island,

is one of many silences. One will creep
like wrinkled sap and globe you in golden sleep.
      Another's crackled by a little
            noise, like an icicle, hard but brittle.

The silence I prefer is as flat as glass;
it magnifies my thoughts when distractions pass
      away like ripples from a clearing
            surface that curious fish are nearing.

THE WORLD OUTSIDE

The world outside has faded with the day.
A while ago, seen through the windowpane,
the yard was all particulars: the chain
holding the swing, the fence-planks that decay

has tilted, flowerbeds, the curving clay
of flowerpots. The world that you could see
by fresher light beyond transparency
was thick with things that you could touch and weigh.

But now, as day diminishes outside,
your lamplit room is twinned. A phantom set
of walls is palimpsested on the grass.

Your mirrored features haunt the cloudy glass
like apprehensions that you can't forget
or memories from which you cannot hide.

CERTAIN DARK

The still life on the table is arranged
with artless art—a plastic water-jug,
a cup of soup, and Jell-O in a mug.
For hours the tableau has been unchanged.
I look at what had been my father once,
dwindling upon a metal bed, and think
of Pharaohs buried next to sustenance
they never touched and wine they would not drink.

The only light in this obscurity
leaks through the narrow crevice of a door.
Revived, some patients claim the dying see
a tunnel slanting to a radiant core,
and figures waiting. Some assert that they
perceived themselves, on table or in bed,
from a perspective somewhere overhead.
I wish I could believe he can survey
this room through other eyes than those that stare
unfocused when I brush the filmy hair
his throes have mussed, or squeeze a brittle hand
that reflex tests against a cotton band.
His soul, I think, would be my age if free,
or younger by six years, as he was when
he saw me first. (I did not know him then;
in this hospital he does not know me).

But no. The luminescent aperture
conceals a bathroom polished to a pure
sterility. The glowing figures, flocked
like angels on a ladder vaguely seen,
ascend a muted television screen.
Behind my father's eyes his soul is locked.

The body is no casing to be shed,
no caterpillar's chrysalis, no mold
shattered by a cicada, nor the shred
of obsolescent self that is unscrolled
across a jagged boulder by a snake.
We are the concentrations of a fire,
fed by decaying timber, flaring higher
between long spells of smoldering in a brake.

The moments when the flame roars to a height—
are they enough to justify the rest?
Our splendor is an episode, at best;
before and after burns uncertain light,
the glimmer of the ember and the spark,
implicated in the certain dark.

III

PARALLEL LIVES

I

Alone together on a somewhere street
        along a mall, when twilight slicks like crude.
A doctor's office, a garage, a fleet
        of eighteen-wheelers that a floodlight's glued
together past a fence. A sign says BAIL
BONDSMAN and makes Kelly think of jail
        and Keith beyond a window, with a pane
        their only link. *You'll never be alone,*
she tells him as, eclipsed, her fingers find
        the glass partition colder than a stone…
She knows what it is like to be confined.

He slouches by her in the driver's seat,
        encapsulated in an amber mood.
He reaches for the dial; the radio's beat,
        a frantic pulse, grows calm. "We shouldn't feud
with your old man," says Keith, his profile pale
as drifting streetlights. "It's just like a sale:
        'This Offer Will Expire.' If I'd've known
        he'd pay my college fees…" At this, a groan
from Kelly. "He's just playing with your mind.
        He treats you like you're something he can own."
She knows what it is like to be confined.

"It's just a trick. The whole thing's a complete
        diversion." Kelly's outburst should conclude
the tense debate. Candescent without heat,
        a pentecost of neon crowns: fast food,
a drive-in bank. "I can't afford to fail
my whole life long"—each word is like a nail
        puncturing her. "You know, he might disown
        you if we go ahead. It's just…I've thrown
away so many years." His words remind
        her of her Dad's. She dreads his altered tone.
She knows what it is like to be confined.

Only when they are knotted on a sheet
        in some hotel room, where a cleanser's brewed
ammonia smells have mingled in the heat
        with his aroma, does she feel renewed.
Only when she reads his backbone's Braille
as they convolve across linen turned stale
        by urgent perspiration and cologne
        can she forget her panic's constant drone.
To think of him and her father aligned…
        This trap is worse than any she has known.
She knows what it is like to be confined.

They pass another mall, an office suite.
     She wishes that her father had been rude,
not understanding. He must not defeat
     her one bid to escape. Keith's attitude
disgusts her. To her now he looks so frail,
as he steers, listening to the radio wail.
     They should have loaded up the car and flown,
     done what her father wants them to postpone.
"It's nothing but a trap that he's designed,"
     she says. "We'll tell him you won't take the loan."
She knows what it is like to be confined.

They curve into the drive-in's pick-up zone.
The kid who passes her an ice cream cone
     is trapped behind his window. In her mind,
as they drive on, she hears his monotone.
     She knows what it is like to be confined.

II (A)

The window is a luminescent slot
     dazzling the guest-room. By the unmade bed
she lingers. Ivory paint looks fresh and wet.

The house—too big for three—stinks with the odd
sharp reek of newness. On the windowsill
like greyish veins the live-oak shadows fall,
      precisely stenciled by the winter sun.
The room's a trap for shadows, drifting in
like minnows that a seine will apprehend.
      This, too, had been arranged, had been foreseen.
She knows that all their choices have been planned.

His voice rings up the stairwell: "Kelly, get
      the keys. They're on the dresser." *Don't keep Dad
and Momma waiting.* The old man has taught
      her husband all too well. He'd let Keith wed
his daughter, treating as collateral
the framed diploma on the bedroom wall.
      He shares his factory outlet with his son-
      in-law—what other boss would hire a man
with Keith's past problems? "*Honey…*" It's that sound
      she's learned to recognize, that stress, again.
She knows that all their choices have been planned.

"If you go to the office, don't forget
      to buy some milk"—the first thing Kelly's said

since leaving home. "Amy will have a fit."
  Keith, driving, answers only with a nod.
The houses pass, most sold, some empty still,
all clean and blank and somehow terrible,
  like spotless cages dripping in the sun.
  Keith says, "I'll go to Safeway. I might win
the lottery." She knows they've been assigned
  a future like the present on and on.
She knows that all their choices have been planned.

The house that Kelly left and yet cannot
  escape awaits them in the shaven yard.
The sound of "Mommy! Mommy!" starts to cut
  the air, a siren, then the small feet thud
and Kelly hoists her daughter in the chill.
"Say hi to Daddy," Kelly has to tell
  the squirming toddler. "Hurry, come on in,"
  her mother scolds the trio on the lawn.
"She'll catch her death of cold out in that wind."
  The Sunday show, on schedule, has begun.
She knows that all their choices have been planned.

The game inside the television set

is blaring through the reupholstered red
garage-turned-den, in which her Dad will sit
    with Keith, the son and heir he never had—
the prodigal, redeemed from drink and pill
and powder, his successor at the mall.
    The HQ, the command post, is the den;
    the kitchen's for the women. "Wipe your chin,"
says Kelly. She lets Amy pour the ground
    cheese on pizza wedges for the men.
She knows that all their choices have been planned.

Dear Daddy, why is it you always win?
You patronize us, just the way you ran
    my life before. We do what you intend.
Her rebel has surrendered. *He* has won.
    She knows that all their choices have been planned.

II (B)

When she gets home, he's watching the TV.
    The crash of keys resounds across the room
on waves of rage. The children run to greet
    their mother—Brian, five, and Bobby, two.

"I drew a dinosaur." "I learned a game
at school today." Exhausted, Kelly feigns
     attention. The apartment smells of smoke.
     The tray is full, each cigarette a toll
exacted for a stretch of squandered time.
     Keith's lost another job. His life's on hold.
She knows without her he could not survive.

"So how was work?" he asks. He oversees
     her sorting of the groceries, gets a new
gold bottle from the fridge. She wants to shriek,
     I never should have run away with you,
my Dad was right. She'd spent the weary day
at yet another agency that paid
     from job to job—so that she could come home
     to this place and replenish the billfold
his dealer-friends would empty, so the lie
     that was their life would not yet be exposed.
She knows without her he could not survive.

"I'm hungry," Brian moans. "You want to eat
     at Burger King?" Keith asks. "Whatever you've
decided," Kelly answers, as he steals

her money from her purse. All afternoon
she labored on the speech that she would make,
imagined the reaction on his face
    to her rehearsed rebukes. Her anger grows
    the way that thunderheads in summer bloat,
accumulating till the flash of strife.
    To think that she had seen him as her hope…
She knows without her he could not survive.

They have this fight each evening. First the screams
    that wake the children, followed by profuse
recanting on both sides, drunken retreat
    into the bedroom, meshing in a spool
of sheets. So often Kelly's vowed to take
the boys and move in with her folks, escape
    this cage forever. But when he would moan,
    "I need you," when he'd phone to say hello
to her at work, she'd know that if she tried
    to leave him by himself he could not cope.
She knows without her he could not survive.

"The least you could have done," she says, "was clean
    this place a little." Keith exclaims, "I knew

there's something I forgot to do." He leads
    the children to the dryer. They remove
the clothes, still warm as rolls to the embrace.
The two boys giggle, as their father drapes
    a sheet across his head. "Look out, a ghost!
    It's got your Mommy!" And then Kelly's throes
turn to a hug. She cannot stop her smile.
    At times like this, she knows she's in control.
She knows without her he could not survive.

The father of her children helps her fold
the laundry. Kelly's father had not known
    she might do more than suffer as Keith's wife.
But she had known, and that is why she chose.
    She knows without him she could not survive.

IV

FOR THE COLD WAR DEAD

It seemed more like a climate than a war.

Not conflict; a condition. An Ice Age
with submarines as floes, and wire moraine,
alliances like glaciers. A great game,
a phony war that had a weather name.

The Cold War. All these years, and I can feel
the winter of that siege's final freeze.
Our stock tank in its crater had congealed.
The snow-slick Brangus mobbed and lowed as we
took turns at chopping through the glassy shield.
The cattle drank. We shivered in the sleet.

Beyond the fence, a few miles to the west
of where we toiled in frozen pasture, spread
the local air force base. When daylight went,
I thought of all the missiles targeted
on Bergstrom in another continent,
pictured a sudden sun that could annex
the skyline where the sun had lately set.

I'm in a terminal, amid the drone
and flash of travellers, gazing on a dome
that irridesces like a skin of soap
over a diorama. "Future home
of Austin's airport—Bergstrom." I'd been told
the base was one of dozens to be closed.
It's still a shock—these model planes in rows,
this temple of a peace we'd never known.

And yet it felt like peacetime all along
way back behind the fronts. Oh, I recall
the Air Force Colonel giving us a talk
in fourth grade, maybe fifth, his chest a vault
of medals; someone's father, he had fought
in Vietnam—that, and the caterwaul
of sirens, in a nursery where we'd squat
beneath our desks like folded, blinking frogs.

But mostly it was black and white TV,
old men in suits, and boy-faced infantry,
the maps and helicopters, refugees
our church had sponsored. Now and then we'd see,
in airports just like this, a young Marine
or G.I. propped against his gear, between
our world and war's. When it was all complete,
there were no triumphs, no solemnities.
For all the legions that did not return,
let this be the parade—the spreading swirl
from terminals to towns across a world
that winter has relinquished. Let it burn.

May runways in remodelled bases boom
as jets go forth to trace their welcome plumes
above Beijing and Moscow, Prague—and, soon,
Havana, and Pyongyang, where gusts of fuel
once lit a prospect cratered like the moon.

JAMAICA

In Jamaica, no grief's allowed.
There the rooftops are smile-white and the terrace pools,
    chairs and shirts are horizon-blue;
laughter's greener and song blacker than dragonflies;
    talk's resilient as hammock string.
Sorrow, though, has a home anywhere people are.
    From the suitcases tourists bring
it will wriggle and slip. It will be swept ashore,
    gripping branches a storm broke off.
I've not visited that island, and yet I'm sure,
    even there in Jamaica, on
afternoons when the blank porcelain dazzle breaks
    into chips on a million waves,
lizardlike on a wall sadness will blink and crawl.

GLIESE 876

Astronomers have discovered two more planetary systems in the universe…In the other system [of Gliese 876], two planets of more normal size are orbiting a small star. The pair of planets are locked in resonant orbits, moving in synchrony around the star…Orbiting objects linked in this way are not unheard of. Three of Jupiter's large satellites—Io, Europa, and Ganymede—travel in such a configuration, as do some of the small satellites of Saturn.

John Noble Wilford, "Found: 2 Planetary Systems. Result. Astronomers Stunned."
The New York Times, Wednesday, January 10, 2001.

We might have known the heavens would provide
similitudes for all relationships
and all events. The image of eclipse
has long evoked the way misfortunes hide

success, the comet the career of pride.
The loved one is the point of the ellipse
that love defines with its concentric trips,
unable, day or night, to turn aside.

Now friendship finally has its metaphor.
These planets orbiting in unison
are surely friends, who can coordinate

the progress of their lives around a core
without the need to make their motions one.
Friends, though independent, resonate.

THE PHOTOGRAPHER'S MODEL

While each successive pose of yours is less
unlike the pose it alters, his finesse
and pliancy of motion grow, the more
he blinds you with the pulsing semaphore.

Already your humanity is drained,
your power siphoned by the one who wields
the camera, your soul already yields
to his dominion. Look, the captor's trained

his captive to respond to chanted words:
you twitch, and twitch again, and then you freeze;
your motions are a puppet's, or a bird's;
you pivot like a lizard by degrees.

Gesticulating, he begins to dance
as bulbs define you with a fusillade.
He is a mate, a monster and a god
to you whom he imprisons with a glance.

MAXIMILIAN'S EYE

In death they granted him an amnesty,
the Mexicans. From cornfield, ranch and town
they came to view the man who'd lost his crown
and then his life. Of rights and sovereignty,
republic, empire, only gentry spoke;
these things were less important than a bride
gone mad and Catholic faith to sandalled folk
who stared at him and prayed for him and cried.

The taxidermist did his duty well;
the lips, they seemed to sigh amid the swell
of golden beard. Only one eye was blue.
The vendors of glass eyes nowhere could find
a second simulacrum in that hue.
With foreign blue and native brown the blind
Germanic dynast stared, as if to show
that he had been absorbed by Mexico.

THE GLASS BLOWER

Melted by blue
fire to glue,
the slack
mash expands,
flexed by a hand's
knack.

Membranes that ooze
in heat like the hues
of crayons,
blown while revolving,
begin evolving
by eons.

Protoplasmic
gel makes phantasmic
coral,
a scaly spore
and flowers and more,
like sorrel

bison and apes
and hominid shapes.
The faces
it makes with a twist
the dexterous wrist
erases.

SEVENTEEN YEAR CICADA

The city seems unchanged
at first—the townhouse row
I pass each morning, cars
and gardens. But I know

something's odd when my step
crackles a papery shell.
The street's encrusted by
cicadas where they fell.

Gold wings, red eyes, black bulks.
Long buried, they must try
to clamber up through soil
and flop and mate and die.

It's June 2004,
a Friday. Since the last
time the cicadas mobbed,
seventeen years have passed.

Seventeen years ago
I was just twenty-five
and far from Washington
and Reagan was alive.

An oriole nabs a bug
in flight. A siren's whine
blends with the choral screech.
Two blocks away, a line

of cars escorts a hearse
to the full cathedral from
the Capitol. The town
to which mourners have come

is one where insects twitch
in clumps on streetlights, walls
and fences. On my sleeve
a black cicada crawls.

In California jets
at sunset dip their wings.
In Washington the night
is full of buzzing things.

THIS AFTER

This after is too long for such a start.
What storm inaugurated should not wane
with shreds and wisps of resurrected rain.
In thunder let what thunder brought depart.

What storm inaugurated should not wane
in textures of a drizzle. What is length
of being unaccompanied by strength?
A cloud resolved at last into a stain.

With shreds and wisps of resurrected rain
the hills are patched. When lightning croaked and gashed
the scaly air, when sky and mountain crashed,
glory was born. Like smoke the fogs remain.

In thunder let what thunder brought depart,
and not in irridescence or the taps
of dimpling silver. Let the sky collapse
again, so that the end will match the start.

THE DEATH OF PINDAR

After a sonnet by August von Platen

When I depart may I fade as abruptly and silently as stars do;
      may death to me come as it did to Pindar.
Not that, in life or in verse, I could ever aspire to match the matchless;
      his death, my friend, I dream of emulating.
Listening, late in a play, to a chorus, in weariness he lowered
      his head upon the knee of his beloved.
After the music had faded, the one who had cradled him said: Waken.
      Already by the gods he had been taken.

No, it isn't a dream. That is a fish, orange with yellow stripes,
gliding over your bed, silent and sleek. Startled to see you rise,
through the window, propelled quickly by blue, shimmering fans, it whips.
Trust me, you are awake. Go and look out; under the window, you'll
see the schools as they drift, silver as faint smearings of fog, around
peddlers parking their carts at their assigned places around the square.
There, that magistrate—see? See how the squid scatter at his approach,
just like pigeons or doves? Look at the way rotating jellyfish
orbit laundry that poor women who woke early today have hung
next to tenements.
                         To you, and to you only, the sea will be
visible. If you told people of what you can perceive, they'd think
you were mad, and indeed, you might agree. Listen to me, the Lord's
own ambassador, this—ocean and earth mingled, the Land of Nod
sunken under the waves, covered by bright water—this really has
happened. Everywhere else where the deluge rolled, the inhabitants
perished, wailing in fear; here in the land founded by Cain alone
folks are going about daily routines, purchasing eggs and fruit
farmers offer at stands, brooming their floors, talking to doctors or
cats or carpenters, not knowing the whole world is already dead.

Yes, the waters will soon drain, and a new race, the descendants of
someone else, will become owners of earth. Forests and animal
life will populate bald chasms today darkened by shadows whales
cast when soaring above. Everyone you know, and the things you love,
though, will crumble before earth is renewed, after this interim
period is complete. It is your fate to be alive between
epochs, one that is gone, one that has not started.

                                            Enjoy this last
day allotted to you. Stroll down the wide boulevards, once again
gaze in awe at the grand statue of Cain, next to the arsenal,
down the block from the shrine. But if you should stop at the tavern, don't
let your neighbors and friends notice that your mood is unusual,
even if, as they tell jokes you have heard dozens of times, a shark
passes. They will dissolve suddenly on learning that they have drowned.

THEY

They are always at their stations among us. Elevated above
the rush of the distracted public,
the occupiers watch us from sentry-posts on monumental
pedestals. The famous dead
are disciplined and self-sufficient. Their flesh is hard, like insect shells.
They never blink or sweat
or sleep or shiver. They gleam like crawfish. Though many, we are not strong
or incautious enough to assault them.

Commemorating their rebellion, we learn not to rebel in turn.
Insurgency was legitimate in earlier
eras; see, they are wearing clothes as archaic as the square obelisks
and domes that they patrol.
The cause for which they fought so nobly was forgotten so long ago
they have grown into what they opposed.

V

THE JUDGE

Screened from the road by tentacular oaks, at the apex of a rocky
        ascent the judge's home was found, a blocky
cottage a pioneer German, a century earlier, made from local
        materials. Above the door, the focal
point was a horse-shoe embedded in limestone, a peasant charm bestowing
        good luck on visitors as they were going
over the threshold. The judge and his wife would unlatch the screen to greet us.
        In summer as in winter, they would meet us
dressed in their finest, as if for a funeral or a Sunday service;
        they'd seat us in the parlor chairs and serve us
tea. Then my brother and I, while the grown-ups were talking, sipped and swivelled
        and watched. The judge was brown and small and shrivelled
like a pecan, in perpetual danger of slowly disappearing
        within the suit from which his face was peering,
stiff as a Halloween mask. Like his features, his voice was unrevealing,
        a drawl communicating all but feeling,
telling my parents the news of the county—a murder or a marriage,
        a business sold, a rancher's wife's miscarriage.

Neither my brother nor I had been born, when my father had collected
        his law degree, and then had been elected
county attorney. The judge of the county had given him direction,
        and, it was clear, a portion of affection.
He and his wife had a daughter, unmarried; their only son, her brother,
        had perished in a car wreck in another

era. The story was told to me later, when I had gone to college.
 The judge's house had in it, to my knowledge,
nothing evoking the boy, no diplomas or photographs. No mention
 of him was made while I had paid attention.
Maybe my father replaced him. My father's own father had been buried
 just weeks before my parents had been married.

All through my childhood the farmhouse, that immigrant pioneer's creation,
 was plagiarized by my imagination.
Each of the cottages housing a woodsman, in fairy tale and fable,
 displayed a weathered orange limestone gable.
When in the pages of Ovid, much later in school, I found the story
 of Baucis and Philemon, in their glory
they were transfigured as live-oaks in front of a house become a temple
 of Texan limestone, small and square and simple.

Once, where a grillwork pilaster and patio ceiling came together,
 a bird attached its nest of twig and feather;
gripping the ladder the judge and my father were holding, stooping under
 the ceiling's rafters, I looked down with wonder
onto the rubbery fledglings that creaked as they jostled in their crater.
 A squirrel I noticed, ten or twelve years later,
next to the patio paused on the tree-trunk to which it had been banished;
 its hazy question mark of tail had vanished.
Hearing me wonder aloud what on earth could have caused it to be missing,

the judge intoned, as if he were dismissing
jurors, "My shotgun."

The rooms in the house were as rich with magic features.
The chairs that seemed like estivating creatures,
poised on mammalian paws, might have risen and ambled right behind you,
unnoticed. Clocks as ancient would remind you,
chiming, that time was advancing—or was it? It seemed as if their series
of clicks arrested time, like a Valkyrie's
vigilant flame or a moat made of thorns or the cave of Rip van Winkle,
from which you might emerge, without a wrinkle,
centuries later.

The stairs to the basement cascaded, steeply winding
to darkness. There we children dreamed of finding
caverns or mines or the den of a troll. From below, a draft ascended,
both cool and humid. When I once descended,
anxious and careful, along with my brother, the judge's wife discovered
what we were doing. Crying out, she hovered
over the stairs to the cellar, abruptly transformed by rage and panic.
The woodsman's wife was now a witch, a manic
ogress who preyed upon children. Our mother collected and removed us,
apologized and angrily reproved us.
She was as baffled as we by the wrath of our hostess. What was under
the floor, the three of us could only wonder.

Fairy-tale figures are ageless. The pair in the woods, however, faded.
　　No spell secured the cottage. Time invaded,
crippling its mistress and stealing her power to talk. She tried to utter
　　a welcome to us, but could only stutter.
Sheltered from sunlight by drapes in the parlor, the judge looked even older.
　　His conversation seemed a little bolder.
He had been reading in Tennyson lately and also in the Bible,
　　and said, with calm indifference to the libel,
he had been waiting for years for a preacher to preach upon the section
　　of Matthew that described the resurrection,
right in Jerusalem, just after Jesus was crucified, of many
　　who left their graves; it seems that hardly any-
body had noticed. The death of a neighbor inspired a somber bout of
　　philosophy: "Whenever you run out of
things to be done, you will die." In the woods, the cicadas started rhyming
　　their stridulation with the wall-clock's chiming.

In a few months he was dead. At the service, beside his speechless wife and
　　his daughter, I reflected on his life and
lore. In the war he had fought in the Navy, then served it for a season
　　in court, a naval lawyer, armed with reason.
Quietly proud of his service, the Judge had once told us he'd refuted
　　the charges brought against a persecuted
sailor. "A Mexican—that was the trouble, behind the whole court-martial."
　　His tone had been disinterested, impartial.

74

Soon, by the grave in the winds of the country, a guard of honor loaded,
      their leader bellowed orders, guns exploded.
Sailors presented his wife with a triangle flag. The distant ocean
      resounded in the lines the Judge had chosen:
Tennyson's "Crossing the Bar." His existence was closed, as he'd intended,
      as each of Tennyson's collections ended.
"He was a father to me!" wept a middle-aged woman to his smiling
      but silent widow. Farmers, teachers, filing
clerks from the courthouse and drillers and fencers had driven through the morning
      to come, with reasons of their own for mourning.
More than a judge, for his neighbors for years he had also been professor,
      accountant, marriage counselor, confessor;
though he preferred to be left to his books and his woods, tradition taught him
      a gentleman must help whoever sought him.

Only a season would pass till the grave of the judge's wife was planted,
      the wish of Baucis and Philemon granted.
Quickly their daughter, unmarried and childless, would follow. With her perished
      the family. A final time, the cherished
horse-shoe lent luck when my father returned and went down forbidden stairs to
      the cellar. Putting all of their affairs to
order, he found what the basement had hidden, among preserves and rusty
      appliances and books grown crisp and dusty.
There in the shadows my father discovered, among the couple's caches,
      the urn that held their son's cremated ashes.

VI

AMERICAN ATHENA

For Audrey Flack

Amid the prickly pear,
where deer by dawnlight flare
      so softly, search.

You'll know the site is mine
on glimpsing, in a pine,
      a hoot owl's perch.

If you have measured well,
in what you've wrought I'll dwell.
      As twilight dims

an eastern butte, my home
will burn with noon and hum
      with fierce new hymns.

IN THE CONFUCIAN TEMPLE IN HANOI

For Nguyen Chi Thien

At first I do not see them, when
I cross the first of two ornate
pavilioned courtyards. Only then
do I notice the rows of great
apotropaic turtles, wardens
bolstering stones, each with the name
of a postulant who came
to be examined in these gardens.

Not crimes accomplished with a sword,
nor tricks a saint or prophet wrought,
but excellence in speech and thought
these old diploma stones record.
Alone almost among the tribes
of earth, this nation honored scribes.

The tablets that the turtles carry
are slabs that fill a cemetery.

CARDINAL BEMBO'S EPITAPH FOR RAPHAEL

Ille hic est Raphael, timuit quo sospite vinci,
Rerum magna parens et moriente mori.

Here is Raphael, whom the parent of everything, Nature,
fearing it would be outdone, feared that it would not outlive.

GENESIS

For Frederick Turner

The earth was incomplete.
The cometary snow
had ceased, as had the heat
that made the granite flow.
Hurricanes had blended
with waterfalls below
the disk of a distended
moon. A phase had ended,

but Earth was not yet made.
Nor was the planet ripe
when forests dripped the shade
of canopies to stripe
a race of reptiles bent
to every size and type.
There remained to be sent
one more ingredient,

the piece that was not used
when ore and ice and stone
originally fused.
The earth should not have grown
without the planetoid
that trailed the sun alone.
For both to be alloyed,
each had to be destroyed.

Concussions wane. The glare
dwindles. A wooded park
is washed by summer air;
beyond the treeline spark
crystalline office towers.
Dogs in the foreground bark,
as joggers test their powers.
Two worlds are one in ours.

I

"The square was dark with orphaned dogs.
They ate the pigeons. One of them begs
still in memory; he was so weak
each time he'd chase a bird, he'd sink."

II

"The harbor smoked. Their shells had hit
the boats. We wept and kept on running.
They'd burned the land, and now they'd set
the sea on fire. The world was burning."

THE SHOOTING AT THE ZOO

A throb of ruby light
from the squad-car, one of a fleet,
is timing the passage of night.
We neighbors, kept from our street,
pace, as detectives meet
and joke. "When will they let
us in?" a lady, upset,
demands. "No-one gets through,"
an officer says. "Not yet."
The shooting at the zoo

took place in the afternoon,
a college student is telling
her phone. "The cop said soon."
Another neighbor's rebelling,
a man whose voice is swelling.
"I'm late!" We're aggravated,
too, but we have waited.
There's nothing else to do
until they've investigated
the shooting at the zoo.

"They said one kid was deceased,"
a guy with a dog explains.
"They bussed them in from Southeast."

That's where the mayhem remains,
most of the time. Bloodstains
on sidewalks we've bought with our rent…
That explains the descent
on Connecticut Avenue
of the legions that failed to prevent
the shooting at the zoo.

Traffic's been diverted.
The lanes that nightly fill
with headlights are deserted.
Veterans of the drill,
photojournalists mill
in formation out
of a van. Rehearsing his pout,
a reporter waits for a cue
to tell the world about
the shooting at the zoo.

Strung through the intersection,
the stripe of flimsy gold
seals the blocks for inspection.
Our exile group's enrolled
a dozen. Dinners grow cold,
children are asking why,

schedules are knocked awry.
Across town, a few
families are crumpled by
the shooting at the zoo.

I look past the tape
at spotlights blocks away,
envisioning the shape
drawn earlier today
to show where a body lay.
It's right that our lives will stall
a moment, when bodies fall;
but then, in one or two
days, we'll hardly recall
the shooting at the zoo.

The moment that it occurred,
each green and yellow bird
in the aviary flew.
The gibbons paused when they heard
the shooting at the zoo.

CIBOLA

Take me to the place of water
where the pyramids are wrought
from the slanted rain, where fountains
pave the very streets they drown.
All its denizens are dreaming,
though they walk among the gleaming
buildings whose facades are streaming
unintelligibly down.

In the city there's an orchard
where mosaic birds explore
labyrinths as checkered, freeing
berries from the bush and tree.
Interlacing boughs are weighing
bubbled fruit as they are swaying
over loops of children playing.
That is where I want to be.

THE BALLAD OF WOODROW WILSON

Tall as the morning, he told the crowd
    from his railroad car:
"The League of Nations is our chance
    to save the world from war."

Columbus and St. Louis, then
    Des Moines. "A heaven-sent
occasion to preserve the peace,"
    declared the President.

In Omaha he had a cough.
    The rocking of the train
prevented him from sleeping all
    across the starry plain.

"America's the savior of
    the world," the towns-folk heard
in Bismarck. On to Cour d'Alene:
    "I give you all my word."

In San Diego he was tense,
    in Salt Lake City terse.
"Without the League, another war
    will come, a war much worse."

At Pueblo, Woodrow Wilson saw
    the children and exclaimed:
"These boys, when they are grown, must not
    be drafted, killed and maimed."

He gripped the railing. "All our boys,
    they will have died in vain
if we should fail…" The curtains closed
    on the departing train.

The waiting crowd in Wichita
    was told the president
was ill. Eastward across the grass
    the locomotive went.

The engine, with a long deep wail,
    dragged the curtained car
over the miles of track that soon
    the boys would ride to war.

THE DEATH OF SENECA

A morning like another.
The slave prepares a bath
and calculates its comfort
with untaught math.

A morning like another.
The barber wipes a blade.
His master eyes its flashes,
unafraid.

A morning like another.
The old man kneels within
the steaming tub's horizon.
Today again

he dictates, true to custom,
as water numbs the scars
and curls of red start rising
toward the stars,

where circumfluent mindfire
is blended from refined
intelligence escaping
the cycle's grind.

A morning like another.

MIDNIGHT TO NOON

Midnight to noon our lives enact the day,
not dawn to sunset. Midnight is the hour
of infancy, bereft like sleep of power
and reason. Childhood is the blur of gray
before the dawn, the gloom that can betray
unfocused senses. Half-awake, we cower
and marvel at the apparitions our
imaginations conjure in their play.

Maturity provides, upon its rise,
its unindulgent light to show us where
we've always been. The world we apprehend
is smaller than we thought. By noon it dries.
Asylum shade is gone. Only the glare
endures, as breezes dwindle till they end.

THE DAY IS AT AN END

The day is at an end.
Around us on the hill
the liquid shadows blend.

Darkness does not descend;
it rises, rather, till
the day is at an end.

While peaks to the east suspend
themselves, the valleys fill.
The liquid shadows blend

together and ascend,
swamping the mountain's frill.
The day is at an end,

and all we apprehend
withdraws. The crickets trill.
The liquid shadows blend.

What day disturbed will mend.
The woods are vague and still.
The day is at an end.
The liquid shadows blend.

Land of the eastering rivers,
though I have chosen to live
far from the prairie your whisper
reaches me nightly in this
neighborhood.

       Under my window
traffic is hissing like wind
filtered by feathery hillsides.
I hear your creeks as they spill
over the chalk, when apartment
heating-pipes gargle and start
clanking.

      A moth's in the lampshade.
Somewhere the harriers ramp.

RETROSPECTIVE

Of all we lived for, most is gone, the rest
will vanish soon. What once we would contest
with adversaries dearer than our friends
will be forgotten. Every struggle ends,
though struggle is unending, every test

gives way to some new challenge. What impressed
us for so long, what drew us to the quest,
the world today no longer comprehends.
                    Of all we lived

to witness, this, it has to be confessed,
is oddest: all the questions we addressed
are asked no more. We need not make amends,
however. Truth, if it exists, depends
on circumstance, but we were true. And best
                    of all, we lived.

BOOKS FROM ETRUSCAN PRESS

God Bless, A Political / Poetic Discourse | H. L. Hix

Chromatic | H. L. Hix | National Book Award Finalist for Poetry, 2006

The Confessions of Doc Williams & Other Poems | William Heyen

Art into Life | Frederick R. Karl

Shadows of Houses | H. L. Hix

The White Horse: A Colombian Journey | Diane Thiel

Wild and Whirling Words: A Poetic Conversation | H. L. Hix

Shoah Train | William Heyen | National Book Award Finalist for Poetry, 2004

Crow Man | Tom Bailey

As Easy As Lying: Essays on Poetry | H. L. Hix

Cinder | Bruce Bond

Free Concert: New and Selected Poems | Milton Kessler

September 11, 2001: American Writers Respond | William Heyen

ETRUSCAN PRESS
www.etruscanpress.org

Etruscan Press books may be ordered from:

Small Press Distribution | 1-800-869-7553 | www.spdbooks.org

Perseus Distribution | 1-800-283-3572 | www.cbsd.com

Printed in the United States
200506BV00002B/1-300/A